Patina of Time

The Hegeler Carus Mansion in La Salle, Illinois

Photographs & Words

by Steve Archer

Copyright @2007 Hegeler Carus Foundation and Steve Archer

All rights reserved. No part of this publication may be reproduced, stored in a retrieval system or transmitted in or by any means electronic, mechanical, photocopying, recording or otherwise, without the prior written permission of the publisher.

ISBN 978-0-9800382-0-0

57 rooms

7 floors

1 family

It's a house, first. It needs a floor, a place to put our stuff down. A roof to cover that goes a long way toward comfort. Walls from down to up complete the box, adding security and seal from the elements — clearing has become shelter.

. . . but after that . . .

This is not a guidebook. Rather it is a set of pictures & words illustrating my experience with this singular home. For those who have walked on its floors, under its roof, within its inimitable walls, it may serve as a worthy remembrance. For those who have not visited, if it drives you to seek out 1307 Seventh Street in La Salle, Illinois, well — nothing could please me more. Never in your life have you seen a house like this one.

Steve Archer

for my family

Illustration by Kevin Peterson, Delineator

As with many historic sites, the Hegeler Carus Mansion has a policy restricting photography. But, when Steve Archer first visited the home in the summer of 2006, his request was so sincere that we struck a compromise — he could take photographs if we could have copies of them. At the time, I had no idea what a providential compromise we had reached.

This book far surpasses any expectations I had that day. Steve has captured the true essence of the home; its warmth, strength, and history. Designated a National Historic Landmark in April of 2007, the home is both a family dwelling and a national treasure.

And, while this is not a guidebook, some factual information about the Mansion seems appropriate:

- Edward Hegeler came to the United States in 1856 with his classmate, Frederick Matthiessen, to form a zinc smelting business, the Matthiessen & Hegeler Zinc Works. The M&H would eventually be the largest zinc manufacturer in the world.
- In 1874, Edward and his wife, Camilla, commissioned Chicago architect W. W. Boyington to design a home for them and their family of seven children. The mansion Boyington designed is a lavish 16,000 square foot, seven-level home which features a mansard roof, dormer windows, molded cornices, decorative brackets and a tower crowned by a 30 foot cupola. The family moved into the home in 1876, and one more child, Olga, was born after they moved in.
- Interior design at the home was done by another Chicago architect, August Fiedler. The Hegeler Carus Mansion is perhaps the most intact example remaining of his interior work and his design here is virtually unchanged since the 19th Century.
- The Mansion was also the birthplace of Open Court Publishing Company, which Edward Hegeler launched in 1887. The goals of Open Court were to provide a forum for the discussion of philosophy, science, and religion, and to make philosophical classics widely available to the pubic. Hegeler hired Dr. Paul Carus as managing editor of the company because Carus shared Hegeler's interest in the relationship between science and religion. Because of his seminal work *The Gospel of Buddha*, Carus is credited with introducing Buddhism to the Western World.
- In 1888, Paul Carus married Mary Hegeler, Edward and Camilla's eldest daughter. They lived in the Mansion with the family and raised their own six children here.
- Mary and Paul Carus's youngest child, Alwin (1901 - 2004) was the last family member to live in the Mansion.

As you might imagine, there are innumerable stories to be told regarding a remarkably intelligent family such as this. These are shared on Wednesdays through Sundays at 12, 1, 2, and 3 PM when the Mansion is open for tours. Please see our website www.hegelercarus.org for more information or phone 815.224.6543.

Sharon Wagenknecht

Oh my, this Hinge.

It was this hinge that brought me to my knees (to see it better)
on my first visit to the house.

It may seem strange, given the other myriad treasures along the way
that might stop me dead in my tracks,

but this Hinge —

It's something to do with the alchemy of form & function,
or rather, function first, then form.

There will be hinges, of course. They will do what hinges do.
But these are stunning,
massive, beautiful.

Who goes to the trouble to make a hinge beautiful, in & of itself?

I knew this house and I would have more than a passing acquaintance.

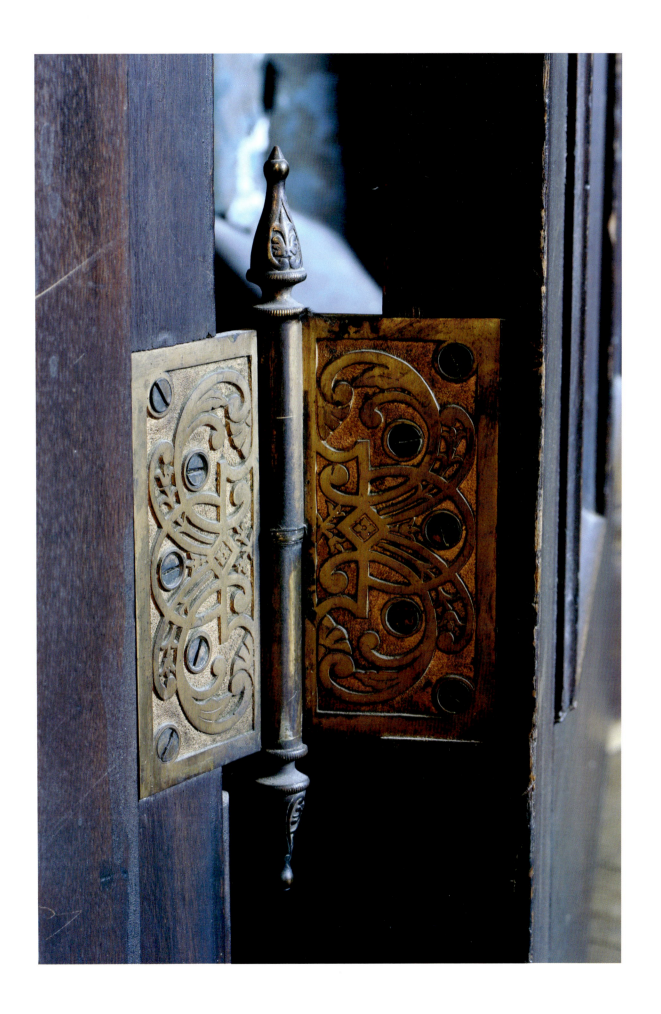

Every Morning on the way down,
every Evening on the way up,
the core of the house, the light that's always lit.

After dinner, and
perhaps
some brandy,
one could aim for it to find the way to bed.

I assure you, the staircase is as solid as any part of the house,
but apparently, even a perfectly sound staircase will develop a list
after a few hundred thousand footfalls.

Sharon Wagenknecht, Executive Director of the Hegeler Carus Foundation, told me
she always walks up on the right side, a method I adopted immediately.

It's going to take us a while to even it out.

A rock solid piece of wood anchoring the family part
of the house
to the public places below.

46,696 mornings at least one right hand
reached for this post on the way to breakfast.

46,696 evenings at least one left hand
reached it on the way to their rest.

Many days & evenings it was 27 or 28 hands.
The downward line of the banister in this shot and the wear evident there
make me happy in the Deep Place.

So much more trouble than they had to go to,
with tremendous effect.
not only an extensively painted motif, but a beautifully molded and
painted triangle attached to it,
with another molded and painted triangle attached to that.
Quite the little mountain.

The molded acanthus leaf motif, born in ancient Greece,
used here beautifully on another ceiling.

The beautiful painted crest entwining Hegeler & Weisbach,
Edward & Camilla . . .
the verticals of the H like two strong trees,
the vine of the W wrapping around.
How happy I am that the two letters are in different "fonts"
but inextricably intertwined.
Everything surrounding the letters is just, well, off the hook.
Someone worked on this, hard.
They earned their iced tea that day.

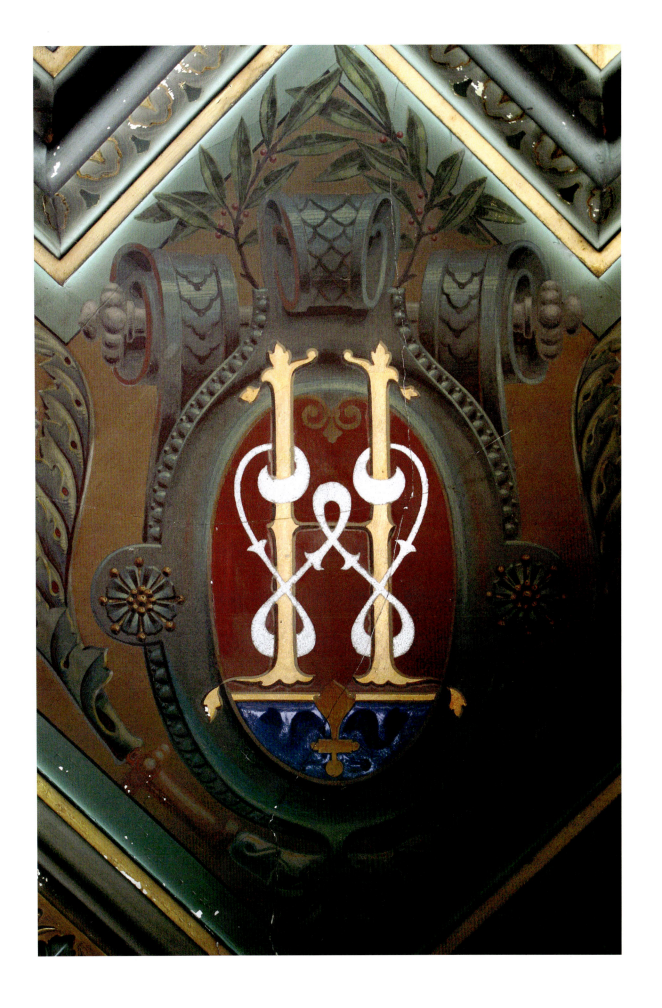

19

Almost completely invisible now, even in the electric era.
I can't imagine anyone got a good look at it in the gas age.
The painter had someone in mind—I wonder who.

The crowning three-dimensional version of the H surrounded by the W
at the apex of the archway into the dining room,
opposite the formal east doors.
What a splendidly impressive and expressive declaration of the union
that brought this all to be.

This thing makes me smile whenever I look at it.
I've never seen anything quite like it.
The kids used to do Shakespeare plays on this wonderful balcony.
It would be an amazing spot to sit and read.
The lamp is an utterly delightful expression
of the happiness I perceived
from the beginning in this home.

If I lived here, it would be lit always.

The hand of the craftsman.
Such things are usually uniform in their appearance—
I felt a thrill as I noted the slightest tremors in the work that was done
to make this mark in the glass
133 years ago.

How on earth did they handle such a massive piece of glass?
What tools did they use? Did they have a compressor? If so, what powered it?
If not,
by hand?—How could that be?

You'll note that the font on the button matches that on the call box indicators.
It instantly became my favorite front door bell button in the western hemisphere.

I won't begin to try to come up with words that attempt to glorify this already glorious vista.
I will say that the veranda and staircase were elements of the house
that didn't withstand the march of time, and have been beautifully restored.
In this case, it is a restoration effort I wholeheartedly applaud.
They've done a superb job.

A tiny excerpt from the lower center of
the remarkable Buddhist shrine in the main hall.

Paul Carus, Hegeler's son-in-law, was instrumental
in bringing the ideas of Eastern philosophy to the Western world.

The presence of this shrine pleases me no end,
and has to figure in the warm chi I feel everywhere within this home.

The one tableau in the book I created—
only by moving the book a few inches to the left to be in the frame.
Open Court is the name of the publishing house started by the family.
They make books to this day.

I truly love this design on a cabinet door in the library.
It appears again in the main hall.

Simple in its line, but complex in the space it describes.

Simply beautiful.

Two of the stunning panels from the bookcase designed by William le Baron Jenney.
Again, the choice of woods, and the artistry used to create
such lovely designs make these truly memorable — fantastic.

If you're in the house as you read this, look very closely at the
dark foundation the designs sit on.

It's wood, too, dark and with an astutely pebbled surface —
an important step that changes utterly the effect of light on the background of the design,
at once laying a lush bed for it and helping it pop out of the panel.

The first thing that caught my eye was the burst of wood in the corner where the vertical and horizontal meet.
Then my eyes were drawn and enthralled by the designs carved in the panels leading to the corner.

Struggled with getting each alone — then just one shot with the burst — then the entirety.
Too complex a composition for me to solve in this century.
Here's what I got.

So old. So used.

Of a configuration at once familiar yet unusual now:

the cradle,

the shape of the spout,

the handle,

the pieces above and aside,

that amazing pepper mill,

the piece of furniture it's on.

It is the entire mansion
captured in a single photograph.

If I ever live in a house that has need of a call box
(and I'm liable to be quite liberal in my assessment of said need),
whether or not it has one,
I plan to have an indicator labeled "Tower".

This piece of furniture represents my introduction to the term "pie shelf",
and will serve as the benchmark against which I'll measure
all others I come across.

I would dearly love to know—
exactly how many pies cooled here?

47

A drawer pull on the cabinet in the butler's pantry.
A lot less would have worked just fine.
This little starburst inside a compass wheel with
surrounding and pervasive botanicals is better.

How many times has it been
opened and closed?
There are much older drawers in the western hemisphere, to be sure,
but most of those are behind velvet ropes by now.

Given the continuous habitation of this house for a century and a third,
without ropes,
might this be the most used drawer on this side of the Pond?

I was overwhelmed when first visiting this house by the warmth I felt within its walls.
Such a huge house, dark interiors, old, tattered —
it should be imposing and, well, cold.
What I felt was just the opposite.
It has to have something to do
with the good chi left by the family who built and dwelt here.
The warm splash of light from this lamp all over this corner is a tangible manifestation.

51

Starch box on starch box on starch box.
This family used starch by the metric ton.
Four family bedrooms, six guest bedrooms, tablecloths,
napkins, drapes, towels, spats.
Laundry was a small industry in this house.

Perhaps laundry was not so small an industry here, after all.
I'm told this massive wheel is part of a machine called a mangle,
used for pressing laundry by passing it between heated rollers.
There were some maids in La Salle in the late 19th and early 20th centuries
who could win a lot of money arm wrestling with the boys.

The motif appears around the chair rail of the entire dining room,
circles the table just under the lip — the table that seats 22 —
every chair back, across the sideboard, the mantle, aped at the picture rail,
made fundamental in the boards of the floor.
Each chair back alone has 120 individual pieces of wood in it — astonishing.

This delightful little wooden flower,
appearing out of the corner of the lovely plant stand in the dining room.
a circle in a circle in a circle.

I asked —
Alwin would take his meals at this table
in this spot, even when he was the only resident,
which he was for 13 years.
The wear on the table there is evident.

That wonderful motif in the dining room,
here in a panel from the fireplace mantle.
I enjoy its every iteration.

I'm a sucker for a good dragon.
This is a great dragon.
The wood choices they made, the comely serrations along his body,
the general curl.
Great Dragon.

65

An astonishing design that I find most compelling.
Sure, it looks a little beaten up by now, but remember
it has borne traffic for 131 years.
I think it's in remarkably good shape, and I would hate to see it
"refinished" in the slightest way.
I like evidence.

Without a doubt the rockin'est fireplace tool I've ever seen or heard tell of. The design in the wood descends from that excellent dragon excerpted elsewhere in the book.

69

The third image in the book of the family room mantle piece.
I suppose that officially makes it my favorite, though I'd hate to choose.

I adore the linear nature of this design —
the burst of life in the center —
the elements sprouting out of the line as it travels —
the interaction with the marble —
and —
and —
and —

For me, one of the most delicate and lovely designs in the entire house.

Three people who saw this photo, independently of one another, remarked "isn't she lovely?"

Yes, she is.

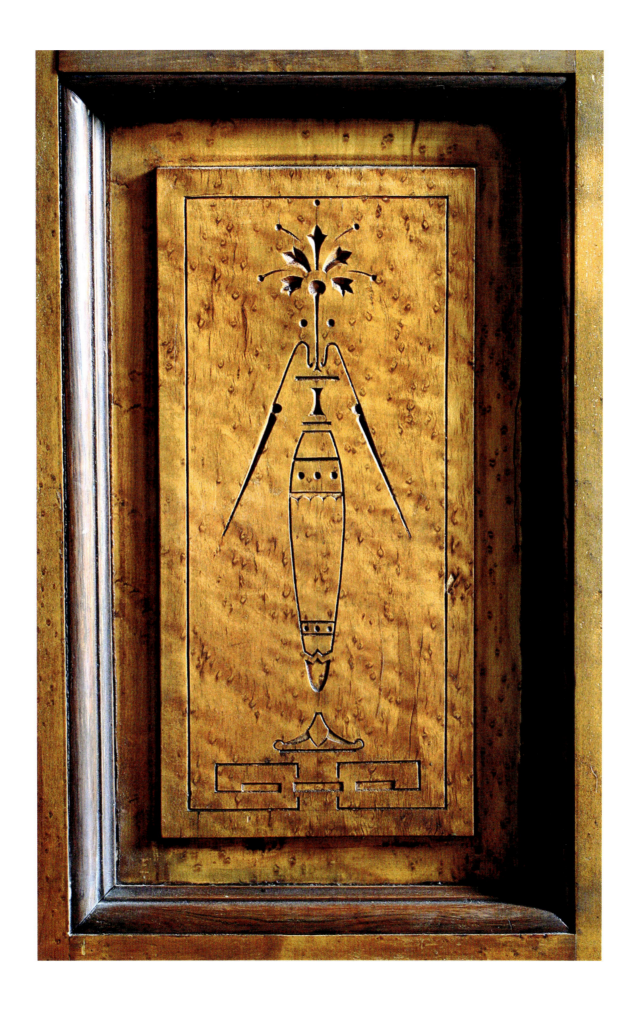

As is so often the case in this beautiful home, the evidence of wear over decades of use takes what already would be attractive into the realm of the fantastic.

It is a lovely design, beautifully executed and expertly placed.
Only a few score trips around the sun could give these tiles their
inimitable patina of time.

Like good music, the rests between the notes as important as the notes themselves.

Like a good Pinter play, the pauses every bit as pregnant and full as the words.

This stylized vine could have had a dozen leaves, or fifty, or a hundred.

It has four.

Perfect.

The presence of wood as important as the places where wood has been taken away.

The walls near the bay window in the parlor,
showing the remarkable shutters found throughout the house.
While they cover the windows from top to bottom when deployed,
they fold away almost magically into the sides of the window,
becoming indistinguishable from the wall itself.

It is a marvelously executed bit of design and functionality.
I never found one that was not in near perfect working order —
most stow and deploy as if they'd been installed last week.

This shot is dedicated to Sharon,
gracious soul who afforded me the opportunity to explore and adore this house.
Thank you, Sharon.

The jade plant's for me.

You have to be standing on this floor to truly see what I love most—

I hope you are or will be soon—

I could not get high enough above it to do it justice with a camera.
An amazing piece of work—
the various shapes transform from boxes to starbursts to etc., ad infinitum.
It is, for me, the crowning floor in the building.

I fell in love with her the moment our eyes met.
I imagine it happens to everyone.
I was stalking her the instant we hit that part of the house.
She's why I wanted to spend an entire day here—
just watching the light change on her face.

I don't know how many shots I took,
trying to capture her essence.
This is the one I've settled on.
I could take as many again without fatigue—it is a joy to do.

It's inconceivable to me that the idea of these faces hanging on
the walls in this house—
this huge, dramatic, old, very lived-in house—
could end up in their actuality appearing anything but . . . creepy,
but they have never seemed anything short of lovely to me.

Lovely in the extreme.

The delicate design above the beautiful wooden face in the parlor, excerpted here to stand on its own, as I feel it does.

The central panel in the parlor mantle.

How many times in a book like this can I use the words

lovely, superb, exquisite, delightful, brilliant . . .

That should exhaust my quota.

There is something I find deeply beautiful in this section of the floor.
It's amazing to see it broken into its component parts—
to see how they put it together—
the trouble they went to—the skill evident.

But beyond that, from a purely aesthetic point of view,
I find it intensely beautiful.
When I visit the house it's the first spot I check,
hoping it hasn't been "repaired".

It isn't about the decrepitude—if you're standing on the floor, you
see there's nothing decrepit about it.
This is the corner by a window under a radiator—
a hundred years down the road it SHOULD be a little worse for the wear.

I hope it stays just as it is.

"The Hegeler Carus Mansion and its collection are a direct link to that which made Illinois a world cultural center in the later 19th century. The treasures of the Hegeler Carus Mansion show it to be the most important survivor of German heritage of its time. This is a unique distinction not only for La Salle and Illinois, but also for the United States."

Rolf Achilles, Art Historian